The Love Is All It Is

Experiencing this life with the angle of
LOVE

Dr Tajinder Kaur

BookLeaf Publishing

India | USA | UK

Made with ❤ on the BookLeaf Publishing Platform
www.bookleafpub.in
www.bookleafpub.com

To all the dark nights

which showed me the light.....

To all the sorrows

And to all the storms I survived...

I dedicate this piece

To the love that I became

going through the darkness of my life...

Acknowledgement

Here I am acknowledging all the phases of my life, which made me what I am today. Surely this life has been the best teacher I could ask for. All my experiences, even though I wanted to get over with some of them, but still they played a big role in my journey.

My parents who always stood by my side and were there with me, who made me capable of creating a better life for myself. I am grateful for my spouse, without whom I wouldn't have learnt to live my life with this vision. My siblings, I love you. And the most important person of my life, my son, he made me a better person just by being there.

To all the friends and the lovely people I met, from whom I learnt a lot.

Thanks Almighty for being there and for supporting me through everything.

I am grateful to BookLeaf Publishing for this opportunity.

I feel there is still a lot more to be thankful for, that is there and that is still coming my way, and I am grateful for everything..

Preface

Life has its own mysterious ways to unfold for us. We never know the true intentions behind the things that happen with us. Sometimes we find ourself in the deep dark moments, that we think are there to finish us, but those times, they carry the power to change the course of our lives in our favour. This I am telling you from my own experience. This book of poetry, that you are going to read has come from such experience.

I never thought of myself as a poet, it never occurred to me to see life in these different colours than what I have been living. A dark night came, through which we struggled, suffered, strived, survived. And it was not a thing of a day or two, it took me years to understand that night and to find my own light. But I can say that event which I used to label the most devastating moment of my life, has given me a new perspective to see this life.

Now here I am becoming the love, writing this piece of my heart with love and for you to see and understand that this life you have been given to find that love in you and to live fully, with all of your heart.

I hope you like this.

Dr Tajinder Kaur

1. The Love Is All It Is

The Love is all it is

You need

You have

You are

What else than this?

The love is all it is

Your dreams

Your desires

Your wishes

And

All your memories

With love they bloom

And with love you succeed

Because

The Love is all it is

Even the story of your life

It's love, which decides

How far you're gonna go

How much you're gonna live

Because

The Love is all it is

This life is sometimes a beautiful cage

With different plays

On different stage

And you find yourself wandering

Sometimes with clarity and sometimes with haze

But you still lose yourself on some days

So to be sane

You need to breathe

And to live this life with all your heart

You need to get out from your mind's slavery

And you have to hold on to this love

As love is the only thing

Which sets you free

Because

The Love is all it is..

2. Countless Stories

Countless stories

Countless roles

There are so many ongoing plays

Being played by the souls

With their shining facades

With their survival armours

They go through this life

Like this is a never-ceasing show

But no

This life has an expiry date

That comes with so many tolls

and yet we waste

every moment in haste

running from now

always desperate

chasing some goals

even though

we know

that we are here just for few calls

and the sad part is

we keep on going

with the same footnotes

living with all the grudges

resentments

and all the woes

refusing to grow

giving it the name of normalcy

we let our stories take control

countless stories

countless roles

why it is so hard

to see beyond

what lies in front of our eyes

what belief this mind holds

why this thing is difficult to realise

that there is a way

there still is hope

for a life that is worth living

a life of growth

you just have to learn

that whatever is yours

it's never gonna go

and whatever left

it never belonged

so live every moment

with all your soul

not chasing

running

but loving

going toward your goals

learn to love

learn to forgive

learn to go with the life's flow

look there is still hope

countless stories

countless roles

with all their thunderstorms and

all their rainbows....

3. Life in the moment

They ask me

what life is?

I say

The moment I am living

with all its colours and its shadows

with all its givings and misgivings

The joy it brings to me right now

and with all the sorrows that I am clinging

Every ride to the sky of emotions

Every visit to the heart of feelings

They ask me

what makes this life easy for you?

I smile and

then I cry

who says it's easy?

it's an emotional roller coaster ride

that I am watching while being alive

I just don't let any moment pass

I stay, I feel, I breathe, I take a deep dive

that doesn't make it easy

but surely a life living worth while

It's all in the moment

that I am perceiving

So life is,

Every moment I am embracing and
Healing.......

4. The Truth

Peace is the destination

And it is the way too

It is also the background

Behind all your emotional blues

You can be happy or sad or be worried

sometimes even with annoyed hues

But with the awareness behind

You can enjoy every view

It's just about having that vision

of knowing that inner truth

That whatever you are feeling

Is not YOU...

5. Silence within

Silence within speaks aloud

To be at home

To be at peace

To be with love

Standing apart from the crowd

Silence within speaks aloud

To feel everything to heal

To cry if there is need

To get it out

To embrace your emotions

Like sky with the clouds

Silence within speaks aloud

To go

To grow

To stand everytime

You fall

To love,

And that's what life is all about

Silence within speaks aloud

It's just you have to tune in to

That emptiness in you

To listen to that music

That's going on in your soul

Without a doubt

That silence within speaks aloud.

6. Black and White

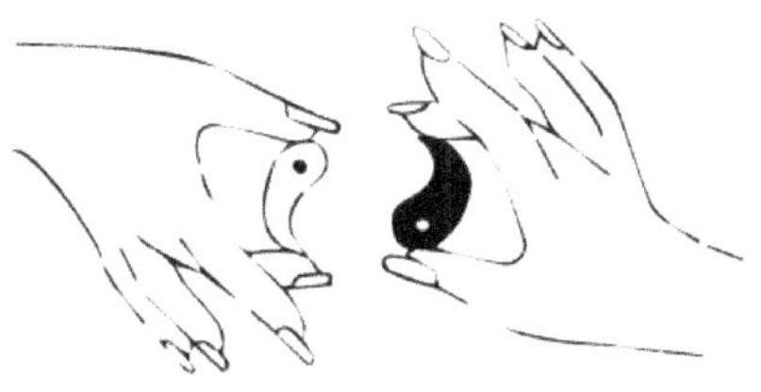

I wonder sometimes

How we take this life

Putting the people we meet

Into categories of black and white

Either they are good or bad

Either wrong or right

This way we decide

Do we need them with us

Or out of our sight

But is it the way?

Because people are not like the day

Or the night

That for the day to rise

The night has to hide

There is always some good in the bad

And some bad in the good

But again this is my perspective

And who knows if I am right?

Some have stories

Some have addictions

Some are just living like sleeping nights

And some with all their dark

Far, far away from their light

So we are here, to divide them into

The disgrace and the knight

There is this notion I want to write

We just have been infused with so much
negativity

And negative all we see,

Is our plight

Let's say

We leave the labels at bay

And learn about the shades of grey

That every being has in them

And they are just trying to survive

Thrive

Just trying to live it right

And we divide them into Black and White...

7. Feel to heal

If you see me sad

Don't ask me to smile

Because I want to feel it all

And be like a child

Who just feel, express, and move on

And love in their own style

And that's the joy it has

To live authentically and being alive

It's sad that we have been taught

To keep these emotions in a pile

To lock them and to hide them

Never show them and suffer

In your own silent cries

You have to be brave enough

You have to be happy enough

In this judgemental world to survive

But is it right?

Little do we know

That these emotions are the thread

To connect the wandering souls

To evolve this human life

The pain that you feel

Is a doorway to your inside

And no one has ever told us

To feel

To go through that pain

To make this life worthwhile

And that is why

I want to live it through

To learn all the clues

To take lessons from my darkness

And shine bright

On another side

So let me be sad

For a while

To live

To laugh with my authentic smile.

8. Just keep flying

I have been here

at this place

and it's been a long time

with so many hopes in my heart

and dreams in my eyes

looking for a launch pad

some opportunity to align

and I sit

and wait

for a sun's ray to come

for me to shine

just thinking of flying..

but how naïve I am being

to have these daydreams

and to sit with this longing

looking for the signs

with the passing time.

and I am thinking of flying

though

this for sure I know

to be that growth

I will have to take the shot

Of flying..

Putting away all my doubts

All the limitations I think about

The chains I have kept around

Leaving all behind

I have to keep flying

Just keep flying

You know,

You have that in you

That zeal to go through

All the hurdles in your view

All the blocks that you harbour in your mind

You have to keep flying

Just keep flying

Taking all the fears of falling

Resting

And restarting, all along

In this journey of being reborn

Creating a life where you belong

With all the freedom in your heart

Without getting yourself tying

You have to keep flying

Just keep flying

With letting your soul free

To be the one with that divine

You have to keep flying

Just keep flying.....

9. Blame Game

What other people did to me

Kept me in the misery

Because I always put the responsibility

Of my suffering

On the other being

Then I waited

For them to rectify

To bring me my peace

And my wings to fly

And I kept waiting

And suffering

Till I realised

This wait will go on

Because who knows

How much time they will take to own

The repercussions of their actions

The responsibility of my suffering

The wounds they inflicted on me

For so long

Just a thought

Will this madness set me free

For the life

I want to live

If I keep waiting for others

To pour into my cup of bliss

You know

Blame game is a dangerous game

It always puts you in chains

Of other people's mayhem

And for sure, whatever you ask or explain

Their actions or behaviour are

Never gonna change

It will keep you stuck

In their pain

And that is insane

As their actions are not because of you

They are maddened with their own traumatic
views

So

You do not need to feel shame

To take the blame

You just need to walk away

To find a way

To transform this unbearable pain

Into the blissful gain

To stay sane

And it will be possible only

If you will take responsibility for your
emotions

If you will own your reign

So rise above the blame

To reclaim

Your growth

Which should be your life's aim

And that surely will change the game.

10. It is fine

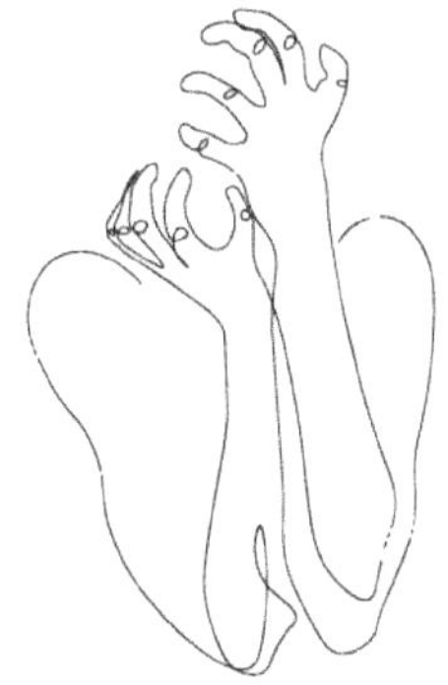

It is okay

To not be fine

To lose yourself

From time to time

To feel sad

To be part of life's rhyme

Because there is pain

And the Reasons to go insane

When life becomes messy and nothing aligns

So it is okay

To lose your shine

Sometimes

But yes

I said

Sometimes

Although

You go

Through many phases of lows

Still there are better days you find

And you don't need to lose yourself for long

In the noise of your mind and

That noise sometimes is not that kind

Yes, you must feel

In order to heal

Whenever something goes out of the line

But you also need to have some space

For the grace

To accept

That there is always some order behind

All that is going that you feel, is unkind

Because everything that happens is already designed

For you and this mankind.

11. Deep wounds

The deep wounds you carry inside

Will give you the vision to see this life

You will numb yourself to every emotion

You will see the chaos even in minimal fights

You will always be on your toes

With the fearful heart and a doubtful mind

And you will keep revolving around

The same unhealthy ground

Carrying along your false pride

The deep wounds you carry inside

Will give you the vision to see this life.

12. Soul's Journey

This soul is still wandering

Looking for its niche

The home she can call it

But surely she is on her way

Sometimes roads are slanting

Leading back to her old place

Leaving her feeling vulnerable

Wanting again to start right away

She has been once the darkness

In fight with herself and all her mates

Always staying in her victimhood

In resistance to everything she face

Then she got the vision of the light

And it was surely the god's grace

And she started her journey

Toward that light

With hope in her prays

She kept falling time to time

Had her doubts and dismays

But she never left the hope

Because she knew that was just a phase

The thing with this path is

That it's a lifelong journey for the soul

With all its downfalls and upgrades

But you have to keep going on

To meet yourself at the higher place

To be one with the order of supreme

To visualise the miracles of this voyage

So she learnt all this from her darkness

And she learnt all this at a loving pace

And she kept going on and on

Toward her better days.....

13. The Space

Going through the dark nights of life

Waiting for the brighter days

With so much chaos inside

We even lose sometimes our ways

Then there is this one question arise

To ask and that's all it takes

Can we manage to see the light in the night?

Can we hold some space?

The space

To uphold all the miseries

All the sufferings and all the bad days

To go all along with it

With the hope in the heart

And the gratitude and the faith

To see the blessings in disguise

To see every downfall with grace

Can we hold the god inside

While walking through that haze?

Can we hold some space?

Then the space for the people

We feel that we hate

Can we remove the filter

Of our perceptions

And reflections

Can we listen to what they say?

Can we be non-judgemental

For all the different ways?

Can we hold some compassion

For the folks we can't even embrace?

Can we see the oneness in all?

The light in all that stays?

Can we hold some space?

And even the space for us

Our faults, our flaws

And our mistakes?

The words we said that hurt

And all the grudges that we reiterate

All the biases that we kept

All the hate that we gave

Can we give ourselves some love?

And then stay with that love always

Can we give some space

To change

To life

To let it unfold in its own ways?

To let it bring all the abundance

The miracles of the grace....

I would say that

Just hold some space

For everything that comes and goes

Through each and every phase

You just be the light and the love

And let this life show you

Your brighter days..

14. The Truth

For years, I tried to find myself in you

Searched for my essence

In the lens, you were seeing through

There was this fog of cultural conditioning

On all of my views

I was this person

Following the crowd blindly

Just walking in the queue

I used to think

That you are only good enough

If your surrounding

If this world validates you

I tried to survive

But always felt deprived

With the cries behind my smiles

And

It shattered me from time to time

Because I couldn't chase the goals

This world made me pursue.

That darkness went on for so long

Until I found my truth

The truth that was there only

Hidden behind the chaotic cues.

I was lost in my own story

In the drama that my mind spewed

And then that truth came to me

When I sat and

Let everything pass through

To meet myself

To renew

With this I came across my soul

My light that I never looked into.

This journey pulled me from my storm

Embracing me with love

A space where I always belonged

It welcomed me to my home

And I became

Like a day

Which always come as new

I still owe everything

To my darkness

To my blues

That made me realise that light

That shines in me and you.

15. The sun does shine

While gazing through the stars

Knowing that it's dark

Tired from all the scars

I know I still have to go far

The path ahead is not clear

But I still have this hope in my heart

And my hope never withers

To embrace a new start

They told me

That this is the hard path

To walk

But still with all the wisdom from my past

I know, a new way I will carve

Right now

I am just breathing

And living, all that is in this moment

And seeing how everything is fine

My heart is beating

And after everything I went through

I am still alive

This life has a way of getting everything done

If you have pure intentions

And a beautiful smile

You just have to wait

And let the universe align

Because

I know for sure

The sun does shine

After every dark night.

16. Hope

It's about time

It flies

Days, months, years pass

Just with the blink of an eye

You laugh sometimes

And

Sometimes you cry

Witnessing the different phases

Of the play of this life

It's easy to lose yourself

With every heartbreak

And every goodbye

I just wish you

Your strength

To keep holding on to your hopes

And

Your smile.

17. The Reality

Was I awake

Or this was some dream?

The more I saw

My eyes wouldn't believe

The fallen kingdom

The ruined beehive

As I walked through it

I was shattered with grief

That storm came

And took everything with it

Leaving me vulnerable

Crying, feeling so weak

Was I awake

Or this was some dream?

Things were a mess

With a havoc beneath

No light in the sight

But I still had this feel

There was this voice of hope

A belief underneath

It's not the end

It is just a bad deed

Things will be fine

We will be fine

Was going on in my mind

On repeat

It's just

You have to breathe and see

This is not what they say

This is not what they feel

This is just a noise

Just a cacophony they scream

Was I awake

Or this was a dream?

You know life is a mirage

It's not exactly the way you see

You see the things

Which these people around want you to see

But you have to have the faith

The courage to believe

That every mess you go through

Is the blessing you need

And there is so much to receive

Even in the chaos

In the harsh breeze

You just have to stay strong in your faith

In the lord's supreme

So I was awake

And it was not a dream

That storm came

To make me a better being.

18. Purposeful life

I have walked a thousand miles

To be the person with a purposeful life

But yet

A lifetime journey is ahead

To evolve

To grow

To unlearn

To touch the sky

And I will take this walk

Through all my lows and highs

With perseverance in the heart

With a resilient mind

To be the person with a purposeful life

The path might be rough

And there might be countless dark nights

But still I will keep embracing the chaos

That surely will be a blessing in disguise

Life is not, what happens to us

It is, what story we write

The story of sorrows, resentments, hatred or grudges

Or story of love, compassion and all the moments that inspire

And I will write

A story of how I loved

And came out of the ashes with smile

To be the person with a purposeful life.

19. Rational or irrational

I am trying to move past

The conundrum of this tug-of-war

Between what I see

Around me

And what I feel in my heart

I know I did some work

Of healing myself

And that work has brought me this far

That I see

Things differently

Not through the lens of this world

Or my ego's selectivity

I see, what is not seen

Nothing, about what my mind is keen

Nor even from my conditioning

But how the things are in reality

And still I know

This might be what my heart shows

And it still can be my subjectivity

But it gives me the sense of peace

Puts all my conundrums at ease

And I flow in this life with love

So let me try a little hard

To move past

The doubts of this mind

To paint my life as art.

20. In the now

Are you here?

In this moment

That is there

Or have you gone back

To some place with regret and tears

And also there is another sphere

Where you go

Someplace far, in your mind

To experience the fear

Are you here?

How lost you feel?

When you are alone

Or even with someone near?

Do you listen to what they say?

To the cries of the heart they share?

Do you stay there?

To be the comfort

To be the listening ear

Or you lose yourself in the noise

Of your mind that is always ready

To interfere.

Do you stay there?

Do you ever acknowledge the beauty around?

Do you enjoy the music you hear?

Do you live every moment?

Do you feel every emotion that appears?

Do you feel the presence of the light in you

Or the others that are there?

Do you live your life to the fullest?

Or you are running around with a stressful
gear?

Can you imagine how you are just going
through life?

Passing every moment

Every day

Every month

Every year

Do you ever slow down to breathe?

Do you ever live in the HERE?

21. As I pause

As I pause

To find the words to say

To listen to the symphony

Of the music my heart create

To be one with this moment

To love

Like I am not gonna get another day

As I pause

I will smile through every phase

I am gonna dance

In every drama, that this life's gonna play

And I am going to stand tall

Be brave

In any failure, in any delay

And

I am gonna rise

Like the life

After every fall and every betrayal

And I will keep going on

And on and on

With faith

And with grace

As I pause

I will learn to pray

Everyday

To show up for myself

Forever and always.

22. Why should I complain

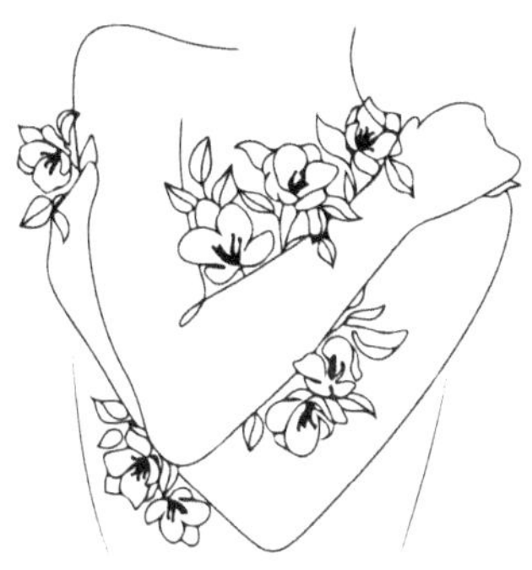

I may have lived

A thousand days

Which at some point,

Were in my prayers

I looked upon

that one grace

Whenever this life

left me astray

I prayed

and there I got

So many ways

I walked

I fell

Then

I got up again

There is so much

I received

Then why should I complain?

Through all my journey

Of those dark days

The thing I learned

That night never stays

It stays until you find yourself

And you understand

That how badly you needed that phase

To grow

To evolve

To love

To have this unshakeable faith

And you learn to stay strong

To go through all your storms

With your brave heart

And a smiling face

Embracing all of life's rainbows

And its rains

Just think

After all this learning

To transform this pain to my gains

Why should I complain?

Why should I complain?

23. Let them be

Let them be broke

Let them be angry

Let them cry

Let them live with their grudges

With resentments

With their fake smiles

It's their journey and

The pace, only they can decide

So it might take a while

Until they realise

Their greatest truth

Of being alive

By knowing their soul

By going inside

And then they will know the real love

And it surely will be their life's greatest mile

Maybe then they will let go

Of their burdened pile

Of all the suffering

That they were enduring their whole life

And then

You would be able to see their genuine smile

Until then

You accept them

As they are

with all their flaws

And their quirky style

Just let them be

Let them sleep

In their dreamy life

You just be with them

With your shining light

Being the guidance in their dark night

So when they find their home

On their own

They can truly know

This life's greatest advice.

So let them be...

24. Just a POV

Sometimes it's just insane

To realise

How casual we have became

Just being insensitive to the emotions of

The dying soul

Crying out in pain

Crying for the life it deserves

For the love it needs to gain

Yes, I used the word 'it'

Because I feel

People are more comfortable

If lifeless it remains

Just for the sake of their taste buds

Just for the greed they contain

I tried to make an argument

With that crying soul

Telling all the reasons I could use

To make this act less profane

Look, Love

Humans have just gone insane

They are not even pardoning their fellows

Torturing, killing them

Just for their substantial gains

And they have their reasons to justify it

And surely very well they explain

But somewhere I knew

All points that I frame

Were pointless and inane

Because this is a life

I was talking about

And

Ending any, is INHUMANE

Those innocent souls will keep crying

For as long as they remain

Because these killings will not end

Until humanity is attained.

25. The choice

Every moment

Gives you a choice

To start afresh

To be here

To accept

To live with the poise

To dance on the tunes

Of the song of your soul's voice

To listen

What your heart says

And to go through this life with complete joy

It's true that

Every moment gives you a choice

To look past

What hinders

To ignore

What annoys

To acknowledge

The way of growth

To create a life

You enjoy

You just have to own your silence

To shut all the worldly noise

Always remember

Every moment gives you a choice

Every moment gives you a choice.

26. Winds of change

No wonder, it's always comfortable

To stay the same

Going through all the ups and downs

With all the stress and the strain

Doesn't matter for how long you have been bound

To the same patterns

To your incessant thoughts chain

You suffer in your mind, endlessly

And

Then in resentment, you inflict that pain

And the irony is

You always manage to find the people

The things or your life to blame

And you feel, it is always alright for you

And everybody to play the same game

The cycle continues for generations and
generations

And then you are always ready for the coming
life

To tame again

But

Can you stop?

Can you wonder?

Can you breathe?

Can you acknowledge the pain,

That it's causing you, to be the same?

Do you want to live your life to the fullest?

Do you want to be in a better frame?

You just have to decide

Can you accept the winds of change?

And truly, this is not for the others

For the outer world

But for the beautiful life, you will attain

For that free mind

For the loving heart

For the contentment, you will obtain

You just have to let go

Let go of your limited story

Your hurting thoughts

Your belief of holding on to pain

You have to surrender

To the new you

To immerse yourself in the loving rain

Break free from everything

That binds you to the chains

Open your arms to a new life

That will be awesomely insane

Just flow with the winds of change.

27. Never-ending hatred song

I wonder

How you take me wrong

When I don't play along

In your never-ending hatred song

I understand that you hold a belief

And I think I know

Where you are coming from

It's not that you have it from the start

It's not that,

You were carrying it when you were born

You saw it

You learned it

You became it

Then with time, it just grew strong

Your never-ending hatred song

And now you try to pass on

To me and to everyone, that you belong

Breaking your heart again and again

And you can't even see

That there is something wrong

You don't even look at me

Through the lens, from what I see

Seeing you struggling so badly

and for so long

And how troubling it is for you to be in these emotions

To fight every minute this chaotic storm

You in your never-ending hatred song

Look

Listen

I just want to hold your hand

Show you the way of love and calm

Make you feel heard, loved all the way

And bask you, in the love

For lifelong

You take your time

And I believe

Time will heal

Your wounds and all your traumas that you
have undergone

But just understand

Let me be

Whatever I want to be

In this journey that is going on

And accept

It is your battle to find yourself

The place you belong

And you will have to do all the work

Even if you have to walk alone

With me by your side

Or even if I am gone

Just understand

I don't want to play along

In your never-ending hatred song.

28. A beautiful world

Our belief is just a limitation

For going beyond the life

Which is in our imagination

A life of freedom

A world with the beautiful sky

Of love

Of laughs

Of a colourful life

Where we can fly

Above all the lies

The lies that surround

The lies that we listen around

Which keep us as prisoners in the walls that
bound

The walls that confound

Us about the humanity

The walls that keep us drowned

In hatred

Our differences

Though we all belong to one sound

The sound which was always there

But we attuned to the glory of fear

The fear of letting our God down

By loving the different ones

On our cultural and religious ground

But you know what is real

Your heart that is always clear

About the love

About that connection

That is lost in this battleground

So we need to listen

To our heart

And that God's sound

Who is there with only one notion

To let go of that limitation

So that we can build that world of
imagination

29. Ask

Do you know who you are?

Without the labels

The titles

The accolades

The tragedies

And your scars

Do you really know who you are?

There are so many stories to tell

So many memories to dwell

The things you achieved so well

And the time you found yourself

Lost in the war

Yet still going on with all that past

Do you know who you are?

Did you even ever ask?

The deep truths

About your soul

Your purpose

About the song of your heart?

Or you just pass

Whining about everything

Through this life

With all that chaos

And all that strife

To reach a point

Which not even ever gonna last.

So ask

About your purpose

About your calling

The rhythm of your heart

To exactly know

Why you are here

And in real

Who you are?

30. Drama of ego

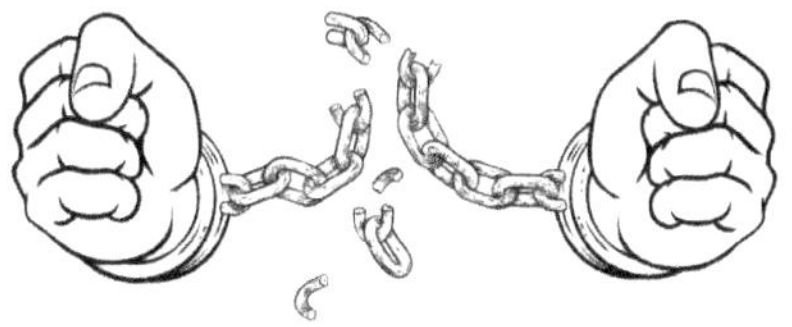

This life is what we have

And with this life we flow

Knowingly unknowingly

We part ways from our heart

And forget the essence of our soul

You know

It is our ego

Which doesn't want us to know

The truth of this life

As it never wants us to grow

The thing it is afraid of

Is love

Because love, makes us lose this ego

So

It creates a false show

That without me

You will always be below

You will always be inferior

From everyone, who are up in the row

And that's what the story is

This ego wants you to know

But my love

The people who have been tricked by its shadow

Only those will go so low

In reality

Not a single soul, here is different

No one is above or below

Only some egos running through this
madness

Who are in constant efforts to make others
bow

To create a world of their benefits

By making you believe that there is just the
hatred

And the chaos

As this love will ruin everything

For them and their goals

Because

Love brings all together

It ends all the drama of this ego

Love makes us realise

Every time

That we are on the same boat

And we all sail in the same flow

This ego doesn't like this

The life without foes

So it doesn't want us to know

The wonders this love does

And how it makes us grow...

So love

Let the ego go.

31. Stay Alive

Stay alive

Even when you don't feel like

Even when you decide

To give up

Even when you think it is a long fight

Just stay alive

Alive in all of the moments

The moments of laughter, love, sadness and even cries

You gotta feel everything

And let everything pass by

You just stay alive

I know it can be hard sometimes

Being lost in the dark

With no light to find

But my love

You have to reclaim your shine

To rise

From the darkest of the nights

So you have to stay alive

Always

Stay alive.

www.ingramcontent.com/pod-product-compliance
Lightning Source LLC
LaVergne TN
LVHW050911200726
843508LV00011B/2176